People who have helped the world

KU-440-398

LECH
WALESA
by Mary Craig

OTHER TITLES IN THE SERIES

Louis Braille by Beverley Birch (1-85015-139-3)
Marie Curie* by Beverley Birch (1-85015-092-3)
Father Damien* by Pam Brown (1-85015-084-2)
Henry Dunant by Pam Brown (1-85015-106-7)
Mahatma Gandhi* by Michael Nicholson (1-85015-091-5)
Bob Geldof* by Charlotte Gray (1-85015-085-0)
Martin Luther King by Valerie Schloredt and Pam Brown
  (1-85015-086-9)
Florence Nightingale by Pam Brown (1-85015-117-2)
Louis Pasteur by Beverley Birch (1-85015-140-7)
Albert Schweitzer by James Bentley (1-85015-114-8)
Sir Peter Scott by Julia Courtney (1-85015-108-3)
Mother Teresa* by Charlotte Gray (1-85015-093-1)
Desmond Tutu by David Winner (1-85015-097-7)
Raoul Wallenberg by Michael Nicholson and David Winner
  (1-85015-109-1)
Coming Soon
Robert Baden-Powell by Julia Courtney (1-85015-180-6)
The Dalai Lama by Christopher Gibb (1-85015-141-5)
Maria Montessori by Michael Pollard (1-85015-156-3)

Titles marked with a * are also available in an abridged
version with a high-interest level and low reading age of about
9 years.

Picture Credits:
Associated Press: 7, 10, 49; Camera Press: 6-7, 21, Dirk Buwalda 22 (below left), Jan Hausbrandt 27, W. Krynski 36-7, Bob Wales 45 (top); Mary Craig: 11 (top); Dachau Museum: 5; Janina Jaworska, Warsaw: 4; Keston College: 11 (below), 57; David King: 13; Popperfoto: 54; Rex Features: cover, Laski/Setbourn 40, Laski 44, 50; Frank Spooner: Bogdan Borkowski 18 (below), 20, Mark Bulka 31, 32, 33, 34, 37, 42, Thierry Campion 45 (below), J. Czarnecki 24, 25, 43 (both), 58-9, Gamma 51, Chip Hires 55, Klahr 22 (below right), Kok 18 (top), 46 (top), 52-3, François Lochon 16-17, 19, 38, 39, 48, Remis Martin 22 (top), N.S.P./Gamma 56, Jean-Paul Paireault 28, Simon & Francolin 15, Bob Wales 41; Voice of Solidarity: 46 (below). Map drawn by Geoff Pleasance.

I would like to thank the unknown – even to me – Polish writer who was originally writing this book for us. "Josef", as we called our anonymous author, disappeared after having completed only a third of the manuscript. To this person, and the thousands of brave Polish people who have faced danger and imprisonment, I can only give my thanks and the thanks of everyone else who believes in the cause of freedom.
I would also like to thank Mary Craig, the author of *The Crystal Spirit*, the most powerful book about Lech Walesa. She took over and helped us by writing this new and special book for young people. She has donated all her fees from this book to Medical Aid for Poland.

Helen Exley, Series Editor

Published in Great Britain in 1989
by Exley Publications Ltd,
16 Chalk Hill, Watford,
Herts WD1 4BN, United Kingdom.

Design copyright © Exley Publications, 1989
Text copyright © Mary Craig, 1989

British Library Cataloguing in Publication Data
Craig, Mary
      Lech Walesa —
      (People who have helped the world).
      1.   Poland. Trade Unions: Solidarnosc.
           Lech Walesa — Biographies.
      I.   Title.
      II. Series.
      331.88'092'4

ISBN 1-85015-107-5

Series conceived and edited by Helen Exley
Picture research: Kate Duffy and Diana Briscoe.
Editorial: Margaret Montgomery.
Typeset by Brush Off Studios, St. Albans.
Printed and bound in Spain by
Cronion SA, Barcelona.

LECH
WALESA

The leader of Solidarity and campaigner for freedom and human rights in Poland

Mary Craig

Nazi occupation

On September 29, 1943, amid the appalling chaos and misery of the Nazi occupation, Lech Walesa was born in the little Polish village of Popowo. In 1939, Nazi Germany and the Soviet Union had carved up Poland between them in a matter of weeks. For the Poles a period of unimaginable hardship and persecution had begun.

Hitler who, as the world knows, hated the Jews and wanted to be rid of them, also hated and despised the Slavs and wanted their lands for the German Reich. He urged his henchmen in occupied Poland to kill "all men, women and children of Polish race or language" without mercy; and if the war had continued for longer, they might well have done so!

"The Poles will work.", said Hans Frank, the Governor of occupied Poland. "They will eat little. And in the end they will die. There will never again be a Poland." All possible future leaders – which meant anybody who had received a higher education – teachers, clergy, doctors, dentists, writers, journalists, students – were to be liquidated. Meanwhile, hostages were rounded up and shot in their thousands. Blonde and blue-eyed children were kidnapped off the streets and sent to Germany to be brought up as Aryans – the pure, untainted Master Race of which Hitler and his Nazis dreamed.

When the Germans over-ran Poland, Lech's father, Bolek, was living with his wife, Feliksa, and their three small children in a two-roomed, stone hut on a small patch of poor, marshy ground. Their part of Poland was incorporated into the German Reich, and all traces of Polishness were being removed. Place-names were Germanized, Polish flags, books, libraries destroyed, Polish schools closed down. German colonists took over the Polish lands, while the Polish farmers became farmhands or were sent to work as slaves on the German military fortifications along the rivers.

Opposite: The concentration camps set up in Poland, for all who opposed the Reich in any way, or who were considered racially inferior, were the scene of wholesale slaughter. Many prisoners were killed on arrival, others were simply worked to death. Lech's father died as a direct result of his years in a concentration camp. Surrounded by electrified barbed wire fences and watchtowers manned by heavily armed guards and killer dogs, prisoners had little or no chance of escape, except, as one prison commandant told them, "through the chimney". This picture shows Polish prison workers, depicted by a fellow-prisoner.

Top: Execution of Poles in Ustron, Silesia, 1939. When the ill-equipped Polish Army withdrew from Silesia in September, volunteer battalions continued to fight. Volunteers who were captured by the Germans were summarily shot. Eleven million people were killed in Poland – the country that saw the worst loss of life in World War II.

Opposite: Polish youngsters build a road in Germany under strict military surveillance. Many Polish boys and girls were taken from their families, deported and forced to work in this way. The German policy was to work Polish people until they were no longer of use – and then to exterminate them.

"Poland [became] the home of humanity's holocaust, an archipelago of death-factories and camps, the scene of executions, pacifications and exterminations which surpassed anything so far documented in the history of mankind."

Norman Davies, from "God's Playground, A History of Poland" Volume II.

Lech's father arrested

Like most of the Polish peasants, Bolek supported the Polish resistance movement, the Home Army partisans who hid in the forest by day and came out at night to collect food and to sabotage the German lines of communication. By sheltering and feeding the partisans, the peasants risked their lives, and many of them were indeed shot or strung up from lamp-posts for this crime.

Lech's sister, Izabela, nine years old at the time, remembers going into the woods with food, and taking blankets to the men who met secretly by night in the Walesas' cowshed. And she remembers with horror that day in September 1943, just before Lech was born, when the men of Popowo were rounded up. Seeing the soldiers, Izabela and her younger brother, Edward, ran into the forest. When they came out again, their father, Bolek, and their uncle, Stanislaw, had been taken away.

Death and a birth

Many of the men arrested in that round-up were beaten to death during the first few days. Bolek, though badly beaten about the head, survived. He

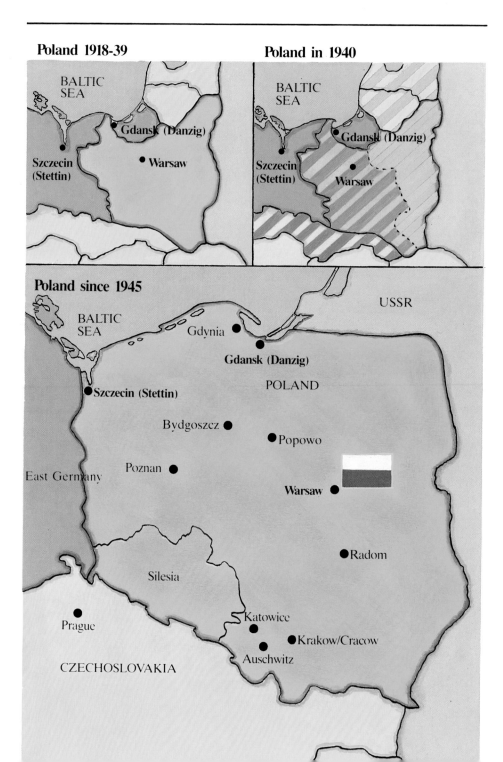

Poland 1918-39

BALTIC SEA

Gdansk (Danzig)

Szczecin (Stettin)

Warsaw

Poland in 1940

BALTIC SEA

Gdansk (Danzig)

Szczecin (Stettin)

Warsaw

Poland since 1945

BALTIC SEA

USSR

Gdynia

Gdansk (Danzig)

POLAND

Szczecin (Stettin)

Bydgoszcz

Popowo

East Germany

Poznan

Warsaw

Radom

Silesia

Prague

Katowice

Krakow/Cracow

Auschwitz

CZECHOSLOVAKIA

was sent off and forced, under constant threat of death, to work – digging trenches and building bridges – while his pregnant wife, Feliksa, was left to look after the farm, three children and her expected baby single-handed.

It was into this unhappy situation that Lech was born. He would never know his father, for in 1945, when the war ended, Bolek struggled home only to die, entrusting Feliksa and the four children to the care of his brother, Stanislaw.

One-fifth of the population of pre-war Poland had been killed in the war, and of these almost 90% had been shot, hanged, or done to death in the concentration camps. Nor were Poland's fortunes about to improve. When the Germans were expelled, the Russians of the Red Army moved in. The Nazi tyranny was immediately replaced by a Communist regime controlled by Stalin in Moscow.

In the post-war years, the countries of Eastern Europe – Poland, Hungary, Rumania, Bulgaria and Czechoslovakia – all became part of the new Soviet empire. And although Stalin had once said that imposing Communism (with its denial of individual freedom) on the freedom-loving Poles would be like trying to put a saddle on a cow, the cow was, under protest, duly saddled.

The ruthless post-war take-over of Eastern Europe by Stalin marked the start of what soon came to be known as "the Cold War" between the Soviet Union and the West. It resulted in both sides entering into a disastrous and expensive arms race.

A pauper childhood

The Walesas were not concerned with politics; their energies were devoted to merely surviving. "We weren't just poor, we were paupers," said one of Lech's brothers. A year after Bolek's death, his brother, Stanislaw, had married Feliksa and they had three children of their own.

So there were two adults and seven children in that tiny cottage with its earthen floor, two rooms and no electricity. Life was very difficult. Stanislaw didn't have much luck with farming his piece of

"Almost certainly for political reasons, the world has learned little to this day of Russia's part in the crucifixion of Poland. Yet in the first two years of this, one of the most brutal occupations in human history, the savagery of the Russians probably exceeded that of the Germans. The Russians had long experience (in a tradition inherited from the Czars and enthusiastically continued) in the effective application of psychological terror."
Mary Craig, from "The Crystal Spirit".

Opposite top left: Free, independent Poland. After centuries of partial or total occupation, Poland enjoyed independence from 1918 to 1939.
Top right: In 1939, in a secret pact, Stalin and Hitler divided Poland into two. This 1940 map shows Russian-occupied Poland to the east and German-occupied Poland to the west.
Bottom: At the end of World War II, Poland was Poland again. But, as part of the cynical Yalta agreement, she became part of the communist dominated Eastern Bloc. For the last forty years, Poland has been neither free nor independent.

Harvesting in Peace, 1945. The war is over at last, the Germans have been driven out by the Red Army, and life returns to a semblance of normality for Poland's largely-peasant population. (Industrialization has not yet begun.) Here, on a farm near the former border with East Prussia, farmworkers gather in the first harvest for six years.

"In one sense we had nothing, but you can't judge poverty by material standards. We weren't well-off, we didn't have television, or even radio, but we had books, and the whole world of nature was open for us to read. We were rich in the things that mattered."

Lech Walesa.

land and found it hard to make ends meet.

The family did not exactly starve, but for the most part their diet consisted of only potatoes, milk and noodles. Buttered bread was a rare treat and very occasionally there was a piece of meat. The children had to tend the geese, take the cows out to graze, weed the ground, make hay and do manual jobs about the house before and after school.

A restless spirit

School was in Chalin, a village about four kilometres away, to which the children walked, usually barefoot, each morning. Lech was better at sports than at academic subjects, though he did not distinguish himself in either. "I didn't really spring into life until the last bell rang," he says, recalling the way he and his friends would play soccer with a home-made ball or fling themselves into the lake near the school to see who could swim the furthest.

Lech, whose surname – Walesa – means "a rest-less spirit", lived up to his name. "He used to go off on his own and think about things more than we did," says Izabela. "He was always different, like the cat who walked by himself."

At school he would argue a lot and get into trouble. "They taught us Communism," he says, "and I didn't pay any attention. Once I was sent to the headmaster and he broke a cane over my head. The trouble was that, if I could see that something or other was white, no one was going to persuade me that it was really black."

At home, Lech was frequently at loggerheads with his stepfather, Stanislaw, a harsh disciplinarian. Feliksa, his mother, on the other hand, had an enormous influence on him. She was a deeply-religious woman, cultured and well-read, with a lively, inquiring mind and a great interest in history and current affairs. All day long she scrubbed, sewed, cooked for the family, gave advice to friends who constantly dropped in to see her, yet in the evening had energy left for reading aloud to her children from the Polish classics.

Thanks to these memories, Lech recalls his childhood as a rich one.

Above: Popowo – The tiny cottage in which the Walesa family lived.

Below: Crosses erected to commemorate the Poznan workers' uprising.

The Polish Revolt of 1956

From his earliest years, Lech was aware of "all the wrongs, the degradations and the lost illusions" suffered by the Polish people. So, in June 1956, although only twelve years old, he was deeply affected when the Poles, hungry, overworked, badly-housed and oppressed, rose in revolt against the Communist regime. (Stalin had died three years earlier, but the repressive system was still in place.) Thousands of workers in the city of Poznan went on strike – and took to the streets calling for BREAD AND FREEDOM. Troops were called out to quell the riots, and many people were killed, wounded, or arrested.

As a result of this violent protest, there was a great upheaval in the country. A new government was formed under Wladyslaw Gomulka, who was installed as leader of the Polish United Workers' Party. Many reforms were promised.

The Polish people called this period their "Springtime in October" and were hopeful that things would now change for the better. They were,

alas, doomed to disappointment, since, for all but the privileged supporters of the regime, life went on being bleak and hopeless.

Trade school

At home in Popowo, Lech Walesa longed to get away from the unrewarding drudgery of farm-work. In the late 1950s, Polish peasant boys were deserting their villages in droves, flocking to the shipyards of the newly-rebuilt and industrialized Baltic Sea towns, like Gdansk and Gdynia.

Yearning to follow their example, in 1959 sixteen-year-old Lech enrolled for a three-year course in mechanized agriculture at the Trade School in Lipno, Popowo's nearest large town. Each week he spent three days getting paid, practical experience in a workshop and three days studying – maths, metallurgy, technical drawing, physics and more general subjects, such as history and Polish. (History, which he didn't consider to have much to do with real life, was always his weak spot!) The money he earned went to paying his hostel fees. Even by Polish standards of those days, Walesa was so poor that teachers and pupils alike felt sorry for him.

He was a quiet, hard-working and determined student. Although an entry in the hostel conduct book complains that Walesa, Lech: "smokes and is a troublemaker", his final report from the trade school assesses his achievement as "fair" and declares him to be "sound in morals and politics". The Director of the school thought him a superb organizer, recalling that when it was Lech's turn to take charge of a weekly work-party to sweep out the school corridors, he needed no advice or assistance from any of the teaching staff.

Military Service

Leaving trade school in the summer of 1961, when he was almost eighteen, Lech spent two years as a mechanic, mending electrical machinery at a State Agricultural Depot near home, before being conscripted into the Polish Army.

He enjoyed his two-year military service away

The Black Madonna of Czestochowa, an icon revered by the Poles as the symbol of their national identity. In 1655, Poland was on the verge of falling to an invading Swedish Army. When the victorious Swedes reached Czestochowa, they encountered some last-ditch resistance: a handful of soldiers gathered around the picture of the Virgin. After an unsuccessful siege of forty days, the enemy withdrew. Amazed by this extraordinary happening, the nation pulled itself together, expelled the foreigner and proclaimed that the Blessed Virgin was thereafter to be venerated as "Queen of Poland". More than three hundred years later, she still is!

A Russian propaganda poster by artist, Dimitri Orlov. The poster supports the position of the communist Red Army and shows a Red Guard stomping on "Polish capitalist oppressors". Across centuries of suffering, Poland had been attacked by Russia to the east and Germany to the west.

from the hard-working poverty of home, won the prize for target-shooting and was made a corporal. "I didn't have any trouble from the men," he recalls. "I managed to get further with them through good humour and jokes than others did through shouting at them." Lech gave lessons in Morse code and ran courses in electricity and radio navigation. In fact he did so well – and liked the uniform so much – that he considered making the Army his career.

But he changed his mind and in 1965 returned home to begin work in another State Agricultural Depot near Popowo. Since Izabela was now married, and Edward and Stanislaw were working away, Lech found himself with all the responsibilities of the oldest of the family. He chafed at the limitations of his life.

At work, though he was known as "golden hands", for his skill at repairing everything from a rusty tractor to a television set or a motor-cycle, he could not even earn enough money to buy the second-hand motor-bike he wanted. And when his girl-friend, Jadwiga, threw him over, he came to a crisis-point. "I was twenty-four and had achieved nothing of any significance. I felt lonely and empty and somehow I knew in my bones that I was in the wrong place."

A one-way ticket to Gdansk

So one afternoon, saying nothing to anybody, he went down to the railway station and bought a one-way ticket to the Baltic coast. As a child, he had once been on a school trip to Gdansk, and it had left him with a lingering memory of the sea – "something vast, stretching out endlessly – possibly freedom." Gdansk spelled adventure into the unknown. So it was to Gdansk that he went, to meet his destiny, far from the restraints and traditions of peasant-life.

In the great Lenin shipyard in Gdansk, Lech Walesa found work as a ship's electrician. It was very different from the rural setting and rusty farm equipment he had left behind, and, at first, he found it strange working with a team instead of on his own. But he soon settled down and for the first time in his life had a taste of freedom. By way of a bonus, he would be able to train on the job as an electro-mechanic.

Hardship and disillusionment

But his actual working conditions horrified him. There was hardly any safety equipment, no changing-rooms, no washing facilities, no drying machines. Men who worked outside in all weathers would frequently go home soaked to the skin. Since most of them began work at six in the morning and the only meal-break was from 9 to 9:15, few could get anything to eat or drink until they returned home at three in the afternoon. As a result, many of them suffered from stomach troubles.

Nor were the hostels much better: "A metal bed-frame with a lumpy mattress, a floor and four grey walls, all filthy and reeking of mildew, a rickety table and two chairs, each missing at least one leg." A man, said Walesa, could eat and sleep in such a

"Our shipyard looked like a factory filled with men in filthy rags, unable to wash themselves or urinate in toilets. To get down to the ground floor where the toilets were took at least half-an-hour, so we just went anywhere. You can't imagine how humiliating those working conditions were."

Lech Walesa.

place, but not really live.

Even though most of the men realized they were being exploited, they were powerless to do anything about it. The trade unions were official Party organizations that existed only to make them work faster and produce more and more for the same wage. "Human dignity and the chance to be fully responsible for one's own life," Lech said, "were not available options."

Slowly, he began to see that whatever changes were made at the top, the workers always lost out. And with that realization came "a deep, irresistible urge to go out and change things". It would not be long before the urge became a passionate life-long political commitment.

Student protests

Trouble began in March 1968 with student riots. That year all over Western Europe students were making some kind of protest, but by and large it was for more power over their own affairs and an end to the traditional way of doing things.

Polish students, inspired by events in nearby Czechoslovakia (where the Stalinist regime had been overthrown and Alexander Dubček, a more liberal leader, installed,) were demanding something much more basic: the right to hold and express opinions of their own. They wanted an end to the deadening official censorship which prevented them from saying, reading or writing anything of which the regime disapproved.

In government eyes, such demands were irresponsible. Three thousand students were arrested, hundreds injured on the streets, hundreds more expelled from their universities with a black mark against their names which would make it impossible for them to get any but the most unskilled jobs in the future. Thirty thousand were sent into exile.

Meanwhile, the brave attempt to establish "Communism with a human face" in Czechoslovakia came to a sorry end when the Soviets and their allies in the Warsaw Pact armies invaded Prague and restored order by force. (To the disgust of most Poles, Polish troops were used in the exercise.)

The Lenin shipyard in Gdansk employs fifteen thousand people. It builds between twenty and thirty ships of 200,000 tons each year – 70% of them for the U.S.S.R.

15

The Soviet leader proclaimed his infamous *Brezhnev Doctrine* that whenever a Communist regime was "threatened from within", the Soviet Union and its allies were entitled to intervene with military force.

Though they had disapproved of the use of Polish troops against the Czech rebels, Polish workers hadn't cared too much about the fate of their own students. Why should they bother about students' lack of freedom when they themselves were hungry and cold?

The authorities tried to stir the workers' indifference into violent hostility by making them attend public meetings at which the students were labelled "spoiled brats" and "hooligans" and blamed for everything that was wrong in the country, including the workers' low wages.

Some fell for this line; Lech Walesa was prominent among those who did not. He and a few friends tried to point out that if the students and intellectuals were being persecuted by the government, that was good enough reason for the workers to support them. It was his first plea for social solidarity – and it failed.

Marriage

If March 1968 marked Lech's first steps into politics, it was important for another reason, too. One day, through the window of a flower-shop in Gdansk, he caught sight of nineteen-year-old Danuta Golós. There had been girls in his life before, but this one was different. A few days later he asked her out, and he courted her for the next year. Like Lech, Danuta was country-bred, from a large family, and she, like him, had dreamed of escape to the big city.

They were married on November 8, 1969, when Lech was twenty-six years old. "We were terribly poor," remembers Danuta, "we were hungry, we

"You don't understand. No one wins against us."
Party boss in Andrzej Wajda's film "Man of Iron".

The presence of Soviet tanks on their soil, and of the Soviet fleet in the Baltic, served to remind the Poles of the ever-present threat of military punishment should they be tempted to step out of line.

17

Right: Empty shelves tell their own story. Shortages not only of food but of almost everything meant that people rushed to buy whatever they could, not knowing when – or if – it might ever be available again.

Opposite: Waiting became a way of life in People's Poland. Women rose before dawn to go into town to be outside the butcher's by six. Then they would wait at another shop for bread, or fish or soap.

Below: It was love at first sight when Lech Walesa met Danuta Golos. She found him "different from other men, both in the way he behaved and in his whole attitude to life". After courting for a year, they were married in Gdansk on November 8, 1969.

had all kinds of problems. But life was very good. I could say it was the happiest time of my life, because Lech and I were always together."

"Something in us snapped"

Life for the Polish people had been getting worse. Food shortages, price increases and low wages meant constant struggle.

Then, on December 12, 1970, the government announced further drastic increases in the price of food and fuel. There was to be no corresponding increase in wages. It was just two weeks before Christmas, the most important family and religious festival in Poland, when housewives were beginning to plan their festive meals. It was the workers' turn to be angry.

Two days later, one thousand shipyard workers surrounded the Party headquarters in Gdansk, demanding that the price rises be withdrawn. No one in authority would talk to the workers, and to the men's fury, they were ordered back to work.

On Tuesday, December 15, the shipyard workers called a strike and twenty-seven-year-old Lech Walesa was elected to the three-man strike committee. With Walesa at their head, three thousand workers stormed the police headquarters, intent

Shipyard workers whose lunch was one lonely sausage each. It was the discovery that shipyard workers were hungry and their working conditions intolerable that gave Walesa "a deep irresistible urge to go out and change things."

on releasing the prisoners held there.

Battles between workers and police broke out all over Gdansk and the authorities declared a state of emergency.

On December 16, men arriving for the morning shift reported that the yard was ringed by army units, with tanks blocking the exit roads. By this time, says Lech, "something in us had snapped. It's hard to imagine how people felt: it was a mixture of despair, desire for revenge and a confused sense of impunity."

No one really believed that the army would attack defenceless workers. But it did. As workers began to leave the shipyard to join the demonstrations, the firing began. That morning four men were killed.

Feelings were running high. Throughout the coastal region, workers downed tools. Ten thousand workers attacked and set fire to the Party building and officials trying to escape were beaten up by the crowd. All day long, the battle raged and by 6:00 p.m., six people had been killed and three hundred injured.

The December 1970 Massacres

As long as they live, the people of Gdansk and its sister-town, Gdynia, will never forget Wednesday, December 16, and Thursday, December 17, 1970. In Gdynia on the morning of the seventeenth, workers were mowed down by machine-gun fire on their way to work and ferocious battles with the police ensued. Hundreds were rounded up and arrested; the dead were buried in secret by night, so that relatives would not know where to find them.

That night, when Lech Walesa finally went home to Danuta and his baby son, Bogdan, he was, for the first time, but certainly not for the last, followed by a secret police "shadow".

The anguish and rage of the Polish people spelled the end of the road for Mr. Gomulka. He was hurriedly replaced as leader of the Polish Workers' Party by Edward Gierek.

For years, Lech Walesa continued to feel guilty of having failed the workers in December 1970.

The subject obsessed him, he brooded on every detail of what had happened and analyzed every mistake. Of one thing he was sure: one day they would be given another chance and when that day came he was determined to be ready.

Gierek's promise

Shortly after Gierek came to power, Lech Walesa was one of three shipyard delegates chosen to meet him. Poland's new leader managed to soothe the angry workers by claiming that, since he had been a worker himself, he understood their grievances well. The meeting ended with his pleading, "Will you help me?" and the workers shouting back, "Yes, we will."

Walesa shouted as enthusiastically as everyone else. In later years he could have kicked himself for being taken in so easily.

At first, once order had been restored to the country, things did seem to improve. The early seventies were the years of détente, when the relationship between the Soviet bloc and the West was more relaxed. Edward Gierek began investing heavily in new industry, modernizing much of the old and importing modern machinery on easy credit terms from the West. The goods produced in the new high-tech factories were to be exported to the West in exchange for the hard currency that Poland needed for the repayment of its debts.

Gierek promised: "a little Fiat car for everyone and decent housing for every family". Suddenly, the Poles, who had been starved for so long of "luxuries" that people in the West took for granted, found themselves able to buy such things as refrigerators, washing machines, transistor radios and television sets. The other, less fortunate, countries of the Soviet bloc were very envious.

Life for women, whether in town or country, and regardless of whether they went out to work, was exceptionally hard. Living conditions were primitive, shortages were chronic, and, unlike Western women, they had almost no modern devices – and no magazines offering helpful tips. Their lives were reduced to the daily grind of: waiting outside shops, hunting, bartering, housework, bargaining and again waiting.

The bubble bursts

Unfortunately, it did not last. When the Arab oil sheikhs raised the price of oil in 1974 and recession and inflation hit the West, there were few buyers

The regime gave priority to state farms and co-operatives, which never made a profit, while starving independent farmers of supplies and technical assistance. For the most part, the peasants went on using horses, as they had no access to tractors. They found it difficult to obtain loans for new equipment, or to get other essentials. Excluded from welfare benefits and harassed by local Party officials, they became alienated.

for Polish products. Gierek was forced to borrow more money from Western banks and used up any remaining profit from exports to repay the interest on the loan. Finally, he had to stop importing and rely on what the Polish factories produced. Almost immediately they began to run out of spare parts for the machines that kept them going.

The consumer boom ended as abruptly as it had begun. Hours waiting outside shops for even the most basic essentials – such as toilet-paper, tooth-paste, razor-blades – became a way of life, and all food was in terribly short supply.

As far as the Gdansk shipyard was concerned, Gierek's changes hadn't amounted to much. True, the yard had been modernized, but only with a view to increasing production and not with the health or safety of the workers in mind. Wages had increased slightly, but working hours were longer than ever, and the work itself was, according to Walesa, "exhausting, inhuman labour that ruins a man's health".

Lech speaks out

To his horror, Lech realized that the shipyard man-agement was gradually getting rid of those who'd been active in the December 1970 strike. He himself was always given the worst jobs and was never allowed any kind of promotion.

One day, in 1976, he could stand it no longer, and decided that, whatever the consequences, he must speak out. His fellow-workers had chosen him as their candidate in the shipyard Union elections. At an election meeting, he furiously denounced the Union as being nothing but "rubber-stamps" for the Party, and accused Gierek of failing to keep any of his beguiling promises.

At the age of thirty-two, Lech had stepped into the arena, and said goodbye to all hope of an easy and comfortable life.

The workers applauded, but the authorities were mightily dismayed. A few days later, Walesa was fired from the shipyard. "Why are they doing this to me?" he cried angrily to a friend. "I don't drink,

"I have always believed that I am the steward of whatever talents I've been given and have to use them to the best effect. I'm an average man … with many faults. I wasn't prepared for great tasks, but life put me in this situation and I have had to do what I can with it."

Lech Walesa.

23

Mother and children living in a seedy two-room apartment. A third of the population were living in the poverty belt.

I'm honest, I come to work on time." He appealed against the dismissal, but in vain. Fortunately he found a new job overhauling cars in the transport section of the Zremb building company.

1976 – Food riots

But already discontent throughout the country was reaching a new boiling-point. In June 1976, Gierek announced that the price of food had to go up (70% extra on meat, for example) and the rate of wage increases to slow down.

Workers at the Ursus tractor factory in Warsaw showed what they thought of that. They tore up the tracks of the Paris-Moscow railway line which ran through the factory, and set up a blockade so that no trains could enter or leave Warsaw.

In the town of Radom, workers attacked the Party headquarters and set it on fire, after first removing huge quantities of food and drink, which the Party élite had been enjoying while the people were almost starving.

The Government reacted violently: the police went on the rampage, laying about the workers with truncheons, killing or arresting them, whether or not they had actually taken part in the demonstrations. Within a few hours, the prisons were bursting and special courts were set up to hand out sentences based on trumped-up evidence and faked photographs.

Predictably, the workers of Radom and Ursus were condemned as "enemies of society" and "hooligans". All over Poland workers were asked, as they had been in 1968 and again in 1970, to denounce such "troublemakers" to the police.

But in Gdansk, Lech Walesa was beginning to realize that, if the workers were to have any hope of survival, they must band together in some kind of solidarity. Under the present system they were denied the right to think for themselves or to express their grievances; and, in Walesa's view, without that freedom to be oneself, human life was scarcely worth living.

Standing up for human rights

Others in Poland were reaching the same conclusion at the same time. The Roman Catholic Church – to which most Poles belonged – was openly championing the cause of human rights and asking for social reform. KOR, an organization of mainly disillusioned former Marxist intellectuals, was set up to bring legal aid to workers unjustly punished after the riots, and financial aid to their families. KOR collected proof of police brutality and judicial corruption – and made their findings known in a variety of new underground publications.

Gierek was livid and ordered all-out war on the KOR group. Its members were harassed, sacked from their jobs, their apartments ransacked, their belongings seized. They and their supporters were regularly attacked, even killed, by the police or by "unknown assailants" who were somehow never found or brought to justice.

But KOR refused to be intimidated. They had realized that the authorities' greatest weapon was the fear they could instil in people's hearts. "Once you can rise above your fear," said Jacek Kuron, a leading member of KOR, "you are a free human being." KOR insisted on acting openly, behaving as though they lived in a free society, lecturing and teaching openly, signing the documents they produced – and accepting the consequences.

The public began to show open sympathy for the KOR group – and to learn from its example. At the same time, the Roman Catholic Church, which had always regarded Marxist (even ex-Marxist) intellectuals with the gravest suspicion, gave them support and insisted on their right to express their views freely. One of the most impassioned protectors of these basic human rights was Karol Wojtyla, the Cardinal of Cracow, soon to become known throughout the world as Pope John Paul II.

A call for free trades unions

On April 29, 1978, Lech Walesa was one of a group of dissident workers and intellectuals who formed a Baltic Committee for Free and Independent

By the late 1970s, the Polish economy had run right out of control. Poland was almost bankrupt, the Western banks had run out of patience, and food supplies were dwindling fast. What food there was was usually of very poor quality. There was a high level of illness among the working population.

Trade Unions. At last he belonged to a group with whose aims he could identify. Avoiding the ever-watchful police, they met in small groups, always in a different place and at a different time, sometimes on a wild stretch of sea-shore, sometimes deep inside a forest.

In spite of all the difficulties and dangers, the group's magazine, *Coastal Worker*, produced a thousand-word Charter of Workers' Rights, signed by sixty-five activists, of whom Walesa was one. It called on workers to throw off their apathy and start looking to their own interests. Only by banding together in independent trades unions could they find the strength to challenge the all-powerful authorities.

Awareness that the police were following his every move – they frequently locked him up for forty-eight hours at a time – did not stop Walesa from cheekily distributing leaflets, posters and copies of *Coastal Worker* in the streets, on trains or in buses. He even handed them out from the pram when he took the baby for a walk! At work he talked openly of the need for a workers' organization capable of defending basic human rights.

Sacked again

Not surprisingly, he was sacked again. Though his angry work-mates threatened a strike, Lech, who now had a wife and four children to support, urged them to be cautious. "Don't make trouble," he advised, "you'll only get sacked yourselves. We're not strong enough yet. But the time is coming when we shall be stronger than they are, and that's when we shall act." What saddened him was that, though his friends resented the system under which they lived, deep down they did not believe that anything could ever change it.

Eventually, in May 1979 he found work with Elektromontaz, an engineering firm producing electrical equipment.

And the police came too! If, for example, Lech went to repair equipment at a building site, they followed on his heels, demanding to know what

When the Polish Pope, John Paul II, visited his homeland in 1979, he received a hero's welcome. He raised the morale of the Polish people and gave them a new sense of solidarity.

On a visit to Auschwitz concentration camp, where many of his own compatriots had died, the Pope laid a wreath on this memorial to the millions of Jewish victims murdered in the camp.

he'd been doing, to whom he had talked, and about what. Possibly because of this obvious harassment, he began to win more and more sympathizers to the cause of free trade unions.

The Polish Pope

To the amazed delight of his fellow-countrymen, Cardinal Karol Wojtyla of Cracow became Pope John Paul II in October 1978. When he visited his homeland in June 1979, he was given a rapturous welcome, and millions flocked to see and hear him.

The Poles were overjoyed that a countryman of theirs had been elected Pope. They believed that this was their reward for all the years of suffering, and they were far more prepared to listen to their

"Be proud of your Polish inheritance. Do not be afraid of difficulties. Be afraid only of indifference and cowardice. From the difficult experience we call Poland, a better future can emerge. But only if you yourselves are honourable, free in spirit and strong in conviction."

Pope John Paul, June 1979.

distinguished fellow-citizen in Rome than to any of the poker-faced men who were their actual rulers. The Pope's visit stiffened Polish morale, and imparted a new, heady sense of solidarity, a new desire for a fresh start.

Remembering the December Massacres

Lech was stubbornly determined to be present for the 1979 anniversary of the December Massacres.

His workmates kept a round-the-clock watch, and when, on the day before the anniversary, a group of policemen arrived at the factory to remove him by force, they smuggled him out in the boot of a small car. Lech went into hiding and did not emerge until the evening of December 16, to join seven thousand men and women at the shipyard gate in a service of remembrance.

Housing conditions were appalling. Young people waited fifteen years for a three-room apartment in a bleak building, where the bath was usually out of order for lack of spare parts. Often, two or three generations lived together in crowded apartments in difficult circumstances.

Walesa arrived late. Being at the back of the crowd, and fairly short, he climbed onto someone's shoulders to make himself heard. It was an improvised speech, but he held the whole crowd spellbound as he spoke of the part he had played in the tragic events of 1970 and of the hopes that Edward Gierek had betrayed.

His words created a powerful bond with his audience, many of whom must have become aware of Lech Walesa for the first time that night. He begged everyone present to organize themselves into groups for their mutual protection. And he ended with a stirring appeal: "Next year, on the tenth anniversary, you must bring a handful of stones to this spot. We shall cement them together and build ourselves a monument."

"Before the war you could see a sign saying BUTCHER and go inside and find meat. Nowadays you see a sign saying MEAT but inside there is only the butcher."
Polish joke.

Out of work – again

The authorities acted swiftly. Next day fourteen men were made redundant at Elektromontaz, twelve of them members of the Free Trade Union groups. Lech Walesa, acknowledged as the company's most outstanding electrician, was among them.

Once again he was out of work – with a family of five to support and a sixth child on the way.

Poland sinks into despair

Poland was almost bankrupt. Food supplies had dwindled and the lines of people waiting outside shops had grown even longer. Women rose before dawn to go into town to be outside the shops by six. If they were lucky, they might get some meat.

Families were living in over-crowded apartments, young people had to wait fifteen years for a three-room apartment in which the bath was usually out of order for lack of spare parts.

As everything continued to get worse, the government assured the people that everything was going splendidly.

Most Poles despised the Party which daily fed them so many lies, and they longed for more honesty and openness.

"It was bad enough that there was next to nothing in the shops. But to raise the price of nothing took the people over the top."
Tim Sebastian, correspondent, speaking on BBC TV, 1980.

Strike at the shipyard

Lech and Danuta's sixth child, a girl (there were already four boys and a girl), was born at almost the same time as Solidarity.

Just as the birth began, the militia came to arrest Lech yet again. Danuta screamed at them to leave him alone. But in vain. Lech returned from his interrogation to find her in hospital with baby Ania. The humiliation of that night went deep. Lech's anger flamed against a system which had so little regard for the dignity of ordinary human beings.

All over the country in that summer of 1980, minor strikes were breaking out in protest against the food shortages and rising prices.

At the huge Gdansk shipyard, the workers were additionally enraged at the sacking of Anna Walentynowicz, just five months before she was due to retire. She was a crane-driver granny who happened to be a dedicated – and very popular – champion of workers' rights and free trades unions.

On the morning of August 14, members of "Young Poland" had distributed leaflets asking the workers to come out on strike for the reinstatement of both Mrs. Walentynowicz and Lech Walesa.

Lech climbs over a wall

Fully expecting to be arrested on the way, Lech Walesa went to the shipyard, walked around to an unused side entrance and was hoisted by waiting friends over a twelve-foot high perimeter fence. It was one of the decisive moments of history.

The shipyard director was standing on a bulldozer truck, arguing with the men. He had almost persuaded them to go back to work. Suddenly, a small, stocky figure appeared on the roof of the bulldozer, towering over him. "Remember me," yelled Lech. "I gave ten years work to this shipyard, and then was sacked. Well, I'm here to tell you we're not going to listen to any more of your lying promises."

As most of the men knew him, at least, by reputation, all talk of returning to work was abandoned. Lech called for an immediate occupation-strike,

and persuaded the workers to elect a committee and work out their demands. At this stage, these were fairly simple: the reinstatement of Lech and Anna; immunity for strikers; a small, monthly pay rise; and (Lech's own obsession, this) permission to erect a monument forty metres high to the martyrs of the 1970 massacre.

Showdown

Next day the other shipyards in Gdansk and Gdynia joined the sit-in strike. It was the start of a full-scale showdown with Poland's rulers, unprecedented within the Soviet bloc. From this tiny beginning grew an inter-factory solidarity strike which in the end would embrace almost the whole of Poland and

August 1980, the Gdansk shipyard. Lech Walesa (seen in the middle of the picture) is the workers' leader during the historic inter-factory solidarity strike which eventually changed the face of Poland. Gates festooned with red and white flowers, Polish flags and pictures of Pope John Paul separate the sit-in strikers from their supportive families and friends.

An improvized Mass attended by 1,500 workers and their sympathizers on the other side of the gate. The Catholic Church had emerged as a powerful champion of human rights in a country where legitimate protest was impossible, and no political opposition was allowed.

"Give over telling us you're sorry,
What guilt for past mistakes you carry;
Look in our faces, weary slaves,
Grey and exhausted like our lives.
"Give over calling us the foe
Of all society, of our brother;
Just count our numbers, and you'll know
How strongly we can help each other....."

From an unofficial collection of young strikers' poems circulated during the shipyard strike, August 1980.

expose the hollowness of the regime's claim to represent the Polish people.

The original short list of localized demands was soon replaced by a much larger one of twenty-one items. It included a demand for an uncensored press, the right to strike, freedom of belief and expression – and, most of all, the right to free and independent trades unions.

The strike committee's manifesto stated clearly: "The workers are not fighting merely for a pittance for themselves, but for justice for the entire nation. We must live up to the immortal words, *Man Is Born Free.*" This was not just a strike but an ethical revolution!

The strikers' demands reflected the whole nation's misery over food shortages, poor medical care, long waiting-lists and the disgraceful inequalities that existed between the privileged few and the vast majority of the people. The workers were seeking not just a fairer deal, but an end to degrading lies and half-truths.

A Solidarity sit-in

As strikers from over five hundred factories joined the shipyard workers, the strike ceased to be a shipyard affair and became a workers' solidarity strike. It grabbed the attention not only of Poland but also of the entire world, and foreign journalists and television crews began to pour in to Gdansk.

It was as though the Polish people had wakened from a deep sleep.

Families and friends could talk to the strikers only through the railings by the gates, gaily festooned with pictures of the Pope and fresh flowers of red, gold and white like the Polish flag. As food was passed in, a team of women cooked and prepared it in an improvized kitchen. Alcohol, by general consent, was banned, and the ban was strictly observed. Strikers slept where they could: on the grass, on cement floors, air-beds, table-tops or sheets of polystyrene.

Lech takes charge

Lech was the hero of the hour. Although the strike was led by an inter-factory committee and was receiving skilled advice from the intellectuals of KOR, it was the shambling, untidy little electrician with the long moustache who seemed to have his finger on the pulse of the strikers. He looked more like Charlie Chaplin than a hero, but he had a natural authority, an instinctive understanding of the strikers' needs and feelings. Lech spoke a language the strikers could understand, light-years removed from the meaningless official jargon in which they were usually harangued.

When things threatened to get him down, he would draw aside to pray. Prayer, said Lech, gave him strength. "I fear nothing and nobody, except God." Every evening in the shipyard there was

"People came from the city by bicycle or on foot; they baked and cooked and carried food and cigarettes. Horse-drawn carts began arriving at the docks laden with potatoes, cabbages, cheese and apples from the farmers. There was even a cart-load of pigs. ... Taxis cruised around, offering transport to anyone bringing food for the strikers."
Lech Walesa.

Lech Walesa has never seen himself as anything but a typical Polish worker. "Go down to the shipyards," he once told the writer of this book. "Talk to anyone there. Every man's story is my story."

Mass, and foreign observers were bewildered at the spectacle of all those thousands of workers on their knees, fervently praying and singing hymns.

The regime gives in

As other industrial cities set up inter-factory committees of their own, and smaller strikes continued to erupt across the country, the regime panicked, realizing it had lost control of the situation.

What was to be done? With the Soviets insisting that matters must not be allowed to get out of hand, Edward Gierek was extremely unwilling to negotiate with an independent strike committee that seemed suddenly to be speaking for the entire Polish work-force. He tried sending a minor official to negotiate separately with representatives of each of the factory units, hoping in this way to divide them. But it was too late for that sort of double-dealing and Gierek was reluctantly forced to send one of his best negotiators, a deputy prime minister for economic affairs, Mieczyslaw Jagielski, to talk with the whole strike committee.

Jagielski and his team arrived in a special bus on the evening of Saturday, August 23, 1980. As the bus reached the yard, a crowd of twenty thousand angry workers surrounded it, shouting "Get out and walk", and "On your knees to the workers". This ugly situation was saved by Walesa arriving to greet the delegation. With considerable skill he calmed the men down, persuading them to let the nervous Jagielski pass unharmed through their ranks.

August 1980, the Gdansk shipyard. With the world watching every move, talks at last take place between the Polish workers and a government team. Every word was relayed by loudspeakers to the crowd waiting outside.

The talks begin

Inside a glass-walled room, with hordes of workers, journalists, observers and photographers peering through the glass, and with every word relayed by loudspeakers to the workers outside, the urbane and neat-suited Jagielski came face to face with Lech Walesa, scruffy as ever.

"These strikes must stop," Jagielski began. "Well, that depends on you," answered the brash little electrician, puffing imperturbably at his pipe.

"Where do you stand on our twenty-one demands?" "Allow me to make a few general points," bluffed Jagielski.

But Walesa was not letting him off the hook. "No, I want a solid answer, point by point."

Those listening outside could hardly believe their ears. In Lech Walesa they had a spokesman who could stand up to a Party bigwig from Warsaw.

A week later the bargaining was still going on. Jagielski had conceded some ground, but on the question of free trade unions he would not budge. The Soviets, meanwhile, were threatening to invade Poland if "the leading role of the Party" in Polish affairs was in any way undermined. Ignoring this blackmail, the miners of Silesia and the steel-workers of Nowa Huta came out on strike and formed their own inter-factory committees.

By then, the strikers in the shipyard were exhausted and desperately anxious about what the government might do next. No one could be sure that the security forces would not move in and start shooting, as they had in 1970.

SOLIDARITY!

Walesa did what he could to keep them calm. When tensions threatened to explode, he would start singing Poland's national anthem – "Poland is not yet dead, so long as we are still alive" – completely off-key, in a cracked, unmusical voice.

"He's a rotten singer, but he can certainly talk," they said.

Yet his growing stature was due not only to his talking skill, but to the fact that he used words honestly, as they were meant to be used. Walesa, calling a spade a spade in rough, ungrammatical Polish, was offering the moral leadership for which Poland was hungry.

By Saturday, August 30, it was clear that by some miracle an agreement was going to be reached. That night, the excited workers carried Walesa shoulder-high to the main gate. They were wearing stickers with the new SOLIDARITY logo that would soon be recognized world-wide as the first independent trade union in the Soviet bloc.

Nationwide support for the strike was almost total. This was no undisciplined, disaffected mob, but an entire people discovering its own solidarity. "We were all friends. We were together at last" is how many people described the phenomenon.

Walesa had his finger on the pulse of the strikers from the start. The chemistry between them was like an electric charge.

The Gdansk Agreement is signed

When the Gdansk Agreement was finally signed on Sunday, August 31, 1980, Walesa, who, though a pugnacious fighter, delighted in former enemies being reconciled, and was jubilant. He saw it as "a success for both sides".

Throwing his prepared speech overboard, he spoke from the heart: "We may not have got everything we wanted, but we got the most important thing, our *independent self-governing trades unions.* That is our guarantee for the future. We have not fought for our own interests but for those of the entire country. We have fought for all of you. And now I declare this strike to be over."

The applause in the hall was echoed by the ecstatic cheering outside. Walesa signed the Agreement with an outsize plastic pen, a souvenir of the Pope's visit, then went outside to be hurled into the air again and again by the cheering workers. Grinning, he gave them a two-fisted salute, shaking both fists in the air like a victorious boxer. "Better this way than a long drawn-out struggle," he said. Then on a more serious note, he added, "But the

next stage will be harder, and I'm a bit scared of it."

He was well aware that the Agreement was only a beginning and that the pitfalls ahead would be daunting. But the majority were more concerned with the triumph of the present moment. No fears for the future could spoil the general euphoria as workers and politicians stood together singing the National Anthem. It was almost unbelievable that such a thing could be happening in a Poland which had been Communist for thirty-five years.

The Agreement represented an astonishing climb-down by the Polish Government. If the promises were actually kept (and that was indeed the sixty-four thousand dollar question), the workers had won for themselves the right to strike; a higher minimum wage; improved welfare allowances. Censorship was to be limited to what was strictly necessary for security purposes; the State radio would broadcast Mass to the nation every Sunday. From now on, managers in all State enterprises were to be chosen because they were right for the job and not because, however sloppy and inefficient, they could be trusted to put the Party's interests first.

Sunday, August 31, 1980. Signing the Gdansk Agreement. On paper, at least, all the workers' demands had been accepted.

*Polish students took to
plastering posters and
political graffiti on the
walls of Warsaw. It was one
of the only ways they could
register their protest. The
dates on this political
poster show the years of
the workers' main
protests.*

Solidarity: the dawn of a new era

Hardly was the ink dry on the paper when word came that Edward Gierek had resigned. For the second time in a decade, a Polish workers' revolt had sent an apparently unshakeable Communist leader packing. Gierek was replaced by Stanislaw Kania, a man of relatively moderate views.

Almost overnight, self-governing unions sprouted all over the country, and before very long Solidarity had ten million members. It seemed as though almost the whole nation was behind it. Even Party members were deserting in their thousands to join.

"It was the dawn of a new era," wrote Lech Walesa in his autobiography. "We felt that after so many years of living upside down, we were at last beginning to walk the right way up."

Enthusiasm positively sizzled as Solidarity (with help and advice from KOR and other intellectuals) began to draw up plans for the transformation of Poland. People sensed their new freedom. For the first time in thirty-five years they could speak their mind without fear. They were stirring times.

Unfortunately, it wasn't like that everywhere. In some places the authorities put every obstruction they could think of in the way of the new unions, refusing to recognize them, (even in some instances to speak to them at all), and issuing dire threats about Soviet intervention.

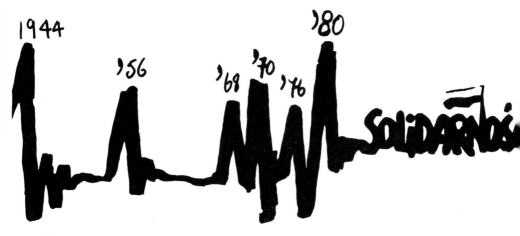

The trouble-shooter

Every day hundreds of people went to Solidarity's Warsaw office for advice and support.

It was Lech Walesa they mostly came to see, the unemployed electrician who was now uncrowned king of Poland.

Lech, sprawled in an armchair and wearing an open-necked shirt and jeans, was given no peace. "They brought him their marriage problems, housing problems, drink problems, everything," said a girl who worked with him at that time. "No one gave him time to think, and everyone expected him to work miracles."

Admiring letters poured in by the sackload for him, crediting him with every kind of virtue, including sainthood. Admittedly there was some hate mail and one or two death threats as well.

Lech, never a modest man, enjoyed the fuss and was flattered by the admiration, but hated having to sit in an office all day long. He had an insatiable passion for journeys and crowds, addressing people all over the country in his crude, slangy Polish, making grammatical mistakes by the ton, contradicting himself constantly, yet holding his audience spellbound by his enthusiasm and refreshing

Lech greeted with enthusiasm by his supporters in Warsaw.

"During the sixteen months following August 1980, for the first time in the history of working-class Poland, we were able to take charge of our own problems instead of being helpless dupes ... in the power struggles of others."

Lech Walesa,
from his autobiography,
"Path of Hope".

honesty. What he called "the ping-pong" of questions and answers exhilarated him.

After meetings he was always ravenously hungry, but not particularly tired, and an hour's snatched sleep in the car going from one meeting to the next was enough to keep his batteries re-charged.

Yet not everyone wanted Lech as leader, now that there was a real possibility of change. His former colleagues on the Free Trades Union committee asked him to step aside for someone more knowledgeable and competent. In their eyes, he was simply not up to the job: he was too soft, too ill-informed, not revolutionary enough in his demands. But Lech knew that the workers wanted him and no one else, and he had no intention of stepping down.

"None of us is beyond reproach"

It wasn't easy to lead a movement of such diversity. Now that the August strike was over, many of the workers were raring to settle accounts with those who'd made them suffer in the past. They wanted to be rid of incompetent or dishonest factory bosses and government officials who'd been feathering their nests for years at the public's expense.

Lech had his work cut out trying to persuade the new Solidarity unions that it was foolish to waste their energies on revenge.

Walesa with KOR adviser, Bronislaw Geremek. During Solidarity's brief heyday, Lech was in great demand as a speaker all over the country. He showed himself to be a man of the people, a people's Tribune rather than a politician.

Lech also had to repeatedly assure a nervous government that Solidarity had no political ambitions and no desire to endanger the Warsaw Pact, the system of defensive alliances with the Soviet Union and the other countries of the Soviet bloc. On the contrary, Solidarity saw its role as that of a necessary permanent loyal opposition, existing only to protect the workers' interests.

The regime strikes back

Sadly, Solidarity's moment had come a little too soon, before the people were really ready to cope with the exciting new concepts of freedom and democracy. Lech was well aware that the unions had no clear policies, they wanted too much too quickly, and were inclined to use him as a scapegoat when things didn't go their way.

They needed time to sort themselves out, but time was not available.

The regime cannily exploited this unreadiness to the full. The faceless men who ruled Poland and who continued to enjoy the privileges of power had no desire to lose those privileges by keeping the promises they had made in August.

As Chairman of the Solidarity National Council, Lech wanted dialogue with the authorities, but found he had to fight them every inch of the way. It took the threat of a nationwide General Strike before he could even get Solidarity officially registered as an independent trades union.

On the day on which Solidarity was finally registered, Lech was the main guest at a triumphant gala of Polish poetry and song at the Warsaw Opera House. His supporters waved banners with legends such as: "Do not be afraid. The whole nation is with you".

But disappointment had already set in, and the workers coped with it the only way they had found to be effective in the past – they went on strike. Lech soon earned the nickname of "the fireman", because he was kept busy dashing hundreds of miles all over the country, putting out the wildcat strikes that seemed to be erupting everywhere.

"None of us is beyond reproach. Are we going to go on for ever settling old scores? Our situation is like that wall over there, if anyone takes just one more brick out of it, it'll fall on top of us. The most important thing right now is for us to get together and create a really effective trade union."

Lech Walesa.

Lech and Danuta asleep on a bus, taking them from one meeting to another. The demands on Lech's time were overpowering, and his private life inevitably suffered. Fortunately, Danuta was an understanding wife.

The Gdansk Monument stands outside the Lenin Shipyard. The three impressive steel crosses, each of them hung with a black anchor, the symbol of hope and the wartime sign of the Polish Resistance, represent the three abortive workers' rebellions of 1956, 1970 and 1976.

"The crosses represent the three workers' rebellions of '56, '70 and '76, the three crucified and unfulfilled hopes.... The monument is tall, because it is a cry to heaven of the people's bitterness."

Anna Walentynowicz,
on the Gdansk monument.

The Gdansk monument

On one issue, the authorities had deemed it prudent to give way. The tenth anniversary of the December 1970 Massacre saw senior members of the government and armed forces standing in driving icy sleet with foreign diplomats, bishops, clergy and one-hundred-and-fifty-thousand ordinary Poles, to unveil the longed-for monument by the entrance to the Gdansk shipyard.

Lech, who always stumbled over a written script, made the clumsiest speech of his life. But it didn't matter. In his eyes the decision to build this memorial was the most important he had ever taken. "Just let them try to knock *that* down," he said, looking proudly at the forty-metre high structure.

But however impressive the ceremony, it represented only a brief truce. The government continued to make promises, then break them again whenever it suited them, and the workers continued to strike as and when they pleased. A new Prime Minister, General Wojciech Jaruzelski, a dour, unsmiling army officer whose eyes were always hidden behind dark glasses, was brought in.

The stage was already being set for the next act of the drama.

Civil war threatens

Matters came to a crisis-point in March 1981 in the small town of Bydgoszcz, where security police broke into a Solidarity meeting and beat up some of its members. There was a huge outcry. Solidarity felt that its very existence was threatened, and began to make plans for a General Strike.

Even among the Communist Party members of Solidarity, support for the proposed strike was widespread. As the countdown began, the air was electric with excitement.

Lech Walesa, however, did not share his colleagues' enthusiasm, since it was obvious to him that the country was about to plunge headlong into civil war.

Just one hour before zero, Lech's efforts were crowned with success and he managed to reach an

Strikes spread across Poland. The top picture shows the capital, Warsaw, paralyzed by a transport strike. And (left) a glass factory, closed by strikers, stands empty. Lech, with no national network of offices and workers, tried to calm angry groups and did his best to coordinate the wildcat strikes.

The family man. Lech and Danuta have eight children, four boys and four girls, two of them, Maria Wiktorja and Brygyda, being born after this photograph was taken. During the Solidarity era and the period of martial law, the six older children, Bogdan, Slawek, Przemek, Jarek, Magda and Ania, knew Lech mainly as an absentee father.

"It was the beginning of the end for Solidarity. It broke our spirit."

A girl in Warsaw.

---

agreement with the Polish government.

Delighted to have "defused an enormous charge of dynamite", he presented this agreement to Solidarity's National Commission – whom he had neglected to consult beforehand.

They were furious with him and almost tearing their hair over what he had done. They believed they had been within an ace of bringing the authorities to their knees; and Lech had destroyed their hopes.

Some of them never forgave him, and to this day feel bitter about his high-handedness and what they see as his betrayal of them.

"I know how far we can go"

Lech, the down-to-earth realist, was unperturbed by the criticism. "I *will* not let things come to civil war," he insisted. "I know how far we can go with our demands. And I know in what country we live, and what our realities are."

He was, of course, alluding to the fact of Poland's inescapable ties to its "Big Brother", the Soviet Union. As the Soviets moved to surround Poland with tanks and warships to the north and east, there were grave fears that they would invade before long.

A travel agency poster in Warsaw suggested wryly: "Visit the Soviet Union before the Soviet Union visits you."

Lech had not been prepared to risk that outcome. But it *was* the beginning of the end for Solidarity. In his heart, Lech knew that the government was preparing for a war to the death. From now on, Solidarity would be living on borrowed time.

Tragedy

Meanwhile, Lech set off to conquer fresh pastures. His first visit was to the Vatican to meet Pope John Paul and to talk with the Italian trades unionists. After that he went to France, Switzerland, Sweden and Japan, "to bear witness to our movement before the whole world." Everywhere he went, he spoke of the need for international solidarity among workers.

The strain of being Solidarity leader takes its toll. Even in his rare off-duty moments (below), Lech is always surrounded by home-grown and foreign journalists and TV crews. "You've become public property, haven't you?" one journalist asked him. "You mean a slave," he countered wearily. "I haven't got a life any more. I'm not living at all."

It was while he was in Japan, on May 13, 1981, that he heard the shocking news of an attempt to assassinate Pope John Paul in Rome. In Lech's horrified eyes, the tragedy of the Polish Pope was the tragedy of Poland – and of Solidarity.

It seemed as though fate was against the Poles.

Anger and despair

The shops were almost bare now. People slept on the roadside all night, so as not to lose their place outside a shop. Potatoes had disappeared completely; meat, sausage, butter, sugar, rice and flour were strictly rationed and often unobtainable.

By imposing martial law on December 13, 1981, General Jaruzelski seemed to the Poles to be declaring war on the nation. After active resistance was crushed, the people resorted to quieter methods. The postal mark (above) gave notice that the Poles had no intention of surrendering. The poster (below) called for the release of Lech Walesa, interned for eleven months in solitary confinement.

Money no longer had any value, and (except in the case of the lucky ones who had access to dollars) bartering took the place of normal buying. There were no cigarettes, matches, or even Poland's national drink, vodka. The factories had run out of spare parts, raw materials and fuels. Hospital patients could not be given food, they had to rely on whatever their relatives could scrape together.

As the Poles got hungrier, their anger grew. People were exhausted by the shortages and the endless hours of waiting in lines for the smallest purchase. The government wasn't even pretending to govern and the country was slithering into chaos. When demonstrations erupted on the streets, the government's only response was to launch a campaign through the media, blaming Solidarity for all the nation's troubles.

At Solidarity's first National Congress in Gdansk in September 1981, nine hundred delegates decided that the time had come to act. Against the advice of Lech Walesa, they called for free elections. They decided to introduce some economic reforms into the factories, and called on workers in the Soviet Union and throughout Eastern Europe to form free trades unions.

Lech told them that they were being wildly unrealistic and maintained that the only real way forward was for Solidarity, the Church and the government to get round a table together and discuss a plan of action – as equal partners.

General Jaruzelski takes over

Solidarity's outburst caused dismay among the politicians and in the Soviet Union. One week later, the moderate but ineffective Party leader, Stanislaw Kania, was replaced by General Wojciech Jaruzelski. The mysterious General in the dark glasses thus became Head of State as well as Prime Minister and chief of the armed forces.

Although the government did not stop baiting Solidarity through the media, on November 4 a meeting was arranged between General Jaruzelski, church leader Cardinal Glemp and Lech Walesa. When this produced no results, the government stepped up its attacks, probably hoping to goad Solidarity into doing something foolish.

The beginning of the end came on November 25 when specially-trained ZOMO riot police landed from helicopters to break up a sit-in by students at the Warsaw Fire Academy. Solidarity once again threatened a General Strike and Walesa summoned his executive to an emergency meeting in Radom.

The meeting-place was bugged. Three days later, Walesa's (carefully-edited) voice was heard proclaiming on Warsaw Radio that civil war could no longer be avoided. In vain did he protest that he had been quoted out of context and that it was the government that wanted civil war. For the first time, the government-controlled media turned on him personally, calling him "a big liar" and a "provocateur", leader of a group of madmen bent on producing chaos.

On December 11, opening a two-day meeting of Solidarity's National Commission in the Lenin Shipyard where it had all begun, Walesa made a last effort to save the peace. "We do not want confrontation," he insisted.

But Solidarity's Commission had had enough and voted next day for a nationwide General Strike on December 17. They were still arguing when reports began coming in of unusual troop movements, of telephone lines being cut off, of Solidarity's headquarters being sealed off, of communications with the outside world being severed.

"Now you've got what you've been looking for,"

"I do what I have to do, regardless of consequences. Obviously, some people will not like it and may decide to put me behind bars. But if you're free inside yourself, it doesn't matter what they decide. The most important freedom is inner freedom, and in that sense I am the free-est man in the world. Nobody is free just to act in his own interest; our human freedom is to act within and for the sake of society."

Lech Walesa.

47

Poland was once again an occupied country, but this time the violators were fellow-Poles. The ZOMO riot police, specially trained and much hated, met all protest against the regime with riot vehicles, tear-gas, water-cannons and truncheons.

Lech shouted angrily and, turning his back on them, he went home.

The General declares war on the nation

As Saturday, December 12, 1981 drew to a close in a furiously whirling snowstorm, General Jaruzelski struck. All Solidarity buildings were seized. In Gdansk, its leaders were rounded up by the security police. As tanks and riot vehicles rumbled through the streets, the police began arresting Solidarity officials all over Poland.

The dream was over.

Solidarity's five hundred days, which had seen the birth of enthusiasm, excitement and new hope, were no more. It was game, set and match to the General.

Early on the Sunday morning, General Jaruzelski told a stunned and grieving nation that he had installed a Military Council of National Salvation in order to save Poland from the chaos threatened by "a handful of reckless extremists".

The Poles were not impressed. By their reckoning, in declaring martial law, the General had declared war on the Polish nation. Nothing would ever shake their belief in that stark fact, and from then on, they referred to what was happening as "the war".

Martial law

All through that terrible day, a military announcer spelled out what martial law would mean; a curfew from 6:00 p.m. to 6:00 a.m.; all gatherings except for church services banned; no more trades unions or student organizations; no public entertainments or sporting events; no right to strike; no private motoring; and all travel by public transport to be greatly restricted. Everybody over the age of thirteen was to carry an identity card and be prepared to be searched, at home or on the streets, at any moment of the day. Telephone conversations were to be monitored, and travel outside Poland was banned. Military commissars were appointed to all schools and universities.

The arrest of Lech Walesa

In the early hours of Sunday morning, riot police, armed with crowbars, came to take Lech Walesa away. He was Poland's unofficial leader and famous across the world, but by dawn he was on his way to Warsaw to begin a year-long internment.

Later that day, the authorities tried to persuade him to appear on television to reassure the Polish people that all was well. He refused.

Solidarity had been taken by surprise and had had no time to organize resistance. But in some places the workers *did* resist, defending their factories and mines against the hated ZOMOs.

On December 16, just a year after the impressive monument had been erected in memory of those who'd been killed in December 1970, tanks stormed the Lenin shipyard in Gdansk. People who tried to get to the monument that evening were dispersed by ZOMOs with tear gas and water-cannon.

Similar incidents were reported all over the country and at the Wujek mine near Katowice,

December 16, 1981. The eleventh anniversary of the 1970 massacres, but in stark contrast to the previous year's ceremonies, ZOMOs broke up the remembrance service with tear gas and water-cannons. In the background is the apartment building from where the first shots had been fired by the military in 1970.

Opposite: May 1, 1982. Nearly 100,000 Solidarity supporters took to the streets to demand the release of Lech Walesa. They were ordinary, peaceful people and their victory was their non-violence. But just hours later the ZOMOs moved in.

Below: Danuta Walesa with baby Ania in 1982. Danuta is a remarkable woman, brave, capable and strong. "She's more of a hero than I am," Lech has said. During the time he was interned, she had to be both mother and father to her large family. She coped, as other women did, with anxiety, poor diet, lack of medicines, high prices and long hours of waiting in line for food.

eight miners were killed by the ZOMOs.

But from the villa outside Warsaw where he was interned, Lech Walesa smuggled out an appeal for non-violent resistance. The Poles were only too glad to respond. Martial law was being carried out with dreadful brutality, and life had become a nightmare.

The six o'clock curfew was violently enforced, and those found out on the streets after that hour were liable to be arrested or even shot. Riot vehicles and tanks were everywhere, and military police seemed permanently to be carrying out identity checks. Telephones were cut off, news broadcasts had once again become a tissue of ridiculous lies.

All those who continued to support Solidarity were sacked from their jobs or, in the case of students, expelled from their schools or colleges.

Non-violent resistance

So the Poles responded to Walesa's appeal for non-violence in various imaginative ways. They stopped buying the official newspapers or watching television. They would go for walks at television news time, or put their sets in front of their windows, the screens facing outward. They listened (as they had listened during the Nazi occupation) to Radio Free Europe and the BBC in order to gain a true picture of how things were.

The silence of Lech Walesa

Most of Lech's imprisoned friends and colleagues in Solidarity were being treated like criminals, confined in rat-infested cells, without proper medical care or hygiene.

Lech's fate was, for the time being at least, more bearable, probably because the regime still hoped to use him for its own purposes. Jaruzelski was trying to persuade him to co-operate with the military regime and abandon his friends. He offered to put him in charge of the new official unions which were to replace Solidarity.

But he underestimated Lech. "I will never bear witness against my friends," he declared. He stood

Solidarity was essentially non-violent. Its supporters' lack of violence was in marked contrast to the way the ZOMOs behaved. On May 13, 1982, several thousand people commemorated the December 13 crackdown. All traffic came to a halt, while pedestrians wearing Solidarity badges stood still with hands outstretched in the V-for-Victory salute. The ZOMOs responded with gas, clubs and cannon. There were heavy casualties and many arrests. The regime described the people who took part in such peaceful demonstrations as "hooligans", "thugs" and "scoundrels".

firm, refusing to recognize the new unions, and insisting that no agreement was possible with the regime, until martial law was lifted and the Solidarity leaders released from prison. Without his colleagues, he said, he had no right to speak, and so would remain silent. From then on, the silence of Lech Walesa became the main symbol of Polish defiance.

Lech was kept in solitary confinement. During this time, Lech and Danuta's seventh child, a girl, was born, but Lech was refused permission to attend the christening ceremony in Gdansk. It was a blow, but not an unexpected one.

Prison gave him time to think and make plans, and taught him patience. "If we fail in what we set out to do, then we have to start again," he decided. "Nothing is ever final. Life is all fresh starts."

Police violence

Opposition to martial law was growing, and General Jaruzelski was ruthless in dealing with it. On May 3, 1982, Poland's national day, ZOMO riot squads wearing masks attacked a large crowd of demonstrators with firecrackers, missiles and tear-gas. On the anniversary of the Gdansk Agreements, reports came in from all over the country, of police opening

fire on crowds of demonstrators, of people being beaten up, of gas-canisters being thrown at groups of women, of schoolchildren being arrested and ill-treated.

According to a poem secretly being circulated, it was as though the government regarded the men in tanks and riot gear as the only honest citizens, while the rest were nothing but "hooligans" and "scoundrels".

The freedom which Solidarity had brought existed no longer. People, including schoolchildren, were constantly being arrested and beaten up. Yet they remained true to Solidarity's belief in non-violence. There were no bombs, no sabotage. To the Poles, such a lack of violence was a deep commitment.

Towards the end of that terrible year of 1981, General Jaruzelski had declared Solidarity illegal, and therefore non-existent. (Solidarity was, in fact, still very much alive as an underground organization, led by a handful of members who'd escaped the round-up of the leaders.)

Perhaps to strengthen the impression that Solidarity didn't count any more, Lech Walesa was released from prison. He was a man of no importance, the authorities said scornfully; he was plain Citizen Walesa.

"It is hard to think of any previous revolution in which ethical categories and moral goals have played such a large part; not only in the theory but also in the practice of the revolutionaries; not only at the outset but throughout the Revolution.... Moreover, it is an indisputable fact that in sixteen months this revolution killed nobody.... This extraordinary record of non-violence, this majestic self-restraint in the face of many provocations, distinguishes the Polish revolution from previous revolutions."
Tim Garton Ash, from "The Polish Revolution".

Walesa comes home

The Poles thought differently. When their hero arrived home from internment on the night of November 15, 1982 a crowd of several thousands waited near his apartment block in Gdansk. WELCOME HOME was painted in huge white letters on the roadside, and banners printed with WE WANT LECH streamed from every window. They shouted for him and refused to let him go. That night he came to the window nineteen times, shouting encouragement to the crowd below, promising, until his voice finally gave out, that he would never betray them.

From now on, he would be closely watched. In fact, he would never again be able to go out without a police escort.

His apartment was bugged and everything he said or did was reported to the authorities. "My telephone and my walls are all ears," he would warn visitors, adding with a laugh, "I am the free-est man in the world. If you're free inside yourself, and say and do what you think is right, you're free no matter what the authorities decide to do."

Early on December 16, when he was due to deliver a speech at the Monument to the victims of the 1970 Massacre, a group of six armed military policemen burst into his apartment and took him away. They drove him up and down for eight solid hours, to make sure that he would not get to the Monument.

But Lech had released his speech in advance to Western journalists. That night, at the Monument, his words were read aloud in his absence. "We have been hurt once again," he had written. "But our cause is still alive, and victory will one day be ours."

Back to the shipyard

Perhaps it was to keep Lech from causing trouble that in April 1983 he was given his old job at the shipyard again. Not long before his fortieth birthday, the man who had been the most important person in Poland, whose face had been known to the entire world, was back to being a ship's electrician.

November 1982, Lech is released from internment and comes home to Gdansk and his family. "I have an old-fashioned attitude to marriage," he says. "A wife's a wife for ever."

"We had, during those 500 days, set in motion an alternative society, while the whole of Poland awakened from its long slumber. We were not the master of our own house; it was and is still ours, but we had returned to the pauper's role, while others in authority again took over. The people had tasted freedom, and now we had to bide our time."

Lech Walesa

It says a lot for his courage and his character that he took it in his stride.

His timetable was exhausting. Up at five in order to be at the shipyard by six, he would find four security policemen always waiting outside the apartment block. Sometimes, if they'd fallen asleep at the wheel, Lech would rap on the car's roof and shout, "Wake up. Time to get going!" One icy winter's morning he even persuaded them to help him get his car started! After work, there were discussions, interviews with the foreign press, meetings with Solidarity advisers. When he eventually reached home, there were more people to see and hundreds of letters from supporters to be answered. He rarely got to bed before midnight.

Meeting with Pope John Paul

Two months after Lech returned to work, Pope John Paul paid a second visit to Poland and asked to see Lech. The authorities didn't want to give such prominence to "this former leader of a former

Reinstated in his old job at the shipyard, the man who had been the "uncrowned king of Poland", admired all over the world, was happy to be an ordinary worker and a family man again.

"I have always been an ordinary worker. It is all I have ever wanted to be. That doesn't mean that I have no ambition to improve myself. But to the end of my days I shall be a working man. And why? Because, in my kind of work, I repair tools old and new, from East and West, from simple hammers to highly complex machines. Now, there's a job to expand a man's mind."

Lech Walesa.

Lech did not go to Norway to collect his Nobel Peace Prize. He was afraid he would not be allowed back if he left the country. Lech's wife, Danuta, and their eldest son, Bogdan, attended on his behalf.

union", and were unwilling for a meeting to go ahead. For the duration of the Pope's visit, the authorities kept a close watch on Lech and didn't allow him any days off work. But the Pope insisted and eventually the two men met for two-and-a-half hours. After the meeting, Lech said, "I felt as though I had received an electric charge ... as though he had passed some of his own peace to me."

In the country at large, things had gone from bad to worse. Food, clothing and medical supplies were so scarce that truck-loads of emergency supplies were being sent in to Poland almost every day from voluntary organizations in the West, to be distributed by the Church authorities.

Hospitals were so over-crowded that children slept in corridors or sat on the floor waiting for beds to become vacant. Doctors and nurses lugged laundry baskets up and down stairs, nurses washed soiled sheets and clothing in hand-basins, and orderlies mopped out the wards without benefit of detergents or disinfectants.

The Nobel Peace Prize

One day in 1983, a friend excitedly telephoned Lech at two in the morning to tell him he had won the Nobel Prize for Peace. Lech refused to believe it, and went back to sleep. Later, as he drove off with a group of friends for a day's mushroom-picking in the nearby woods, his little white car was followed by at least eight taxis full of foreign journalists who'd already heard the rumours. At 11 o'clock, everyone piled out of the cars to huddle over a radio set. When a German station announced that the Nobel Peace Prize had been awarded to Walesa, his friends grabbed Lech's arms and legs and tossed him into the air in triumph. Then they all turned round and went home, to find an excited crowd – and hordes of foreign news teams – waiting for Lech.

In his Nobel speech, which was read by Danuta, Lech claimed that the award was not for himself, but for the heroic achievements of Solidarity which had continued to be non-violent, in spite of the ruthless violence used against it. All his life, he said, he had been surrounded by "violence, hatred and lies", and the lesson he had learned was that "we can effectively oppose violence only if we do not resort to it". The Polish people wanted dialogue, not confrontation, with their government.

The years of repression

Unfortunately, it was a message lost on the Polish government. Though martial law – the Poles continued to call it "the war" – had officially ended in July 1983, the government and people were growing further and further apart.

Walesa's Nobel Prize had little visible effect on the Polish rulers, who continued with their repression while insisting that Lech Walesa was a Polish citizen of no importance whatsoever.

For five years, Poland remained in darkness, waiting for that brave candle of peace to be lit again. Any opposition was met with imprisonment without trial or even murder. Father Popieluszko was just one example of the fate of the bravest. Visitors to Poland described a nation of "no-hopers", in which the only antidote to endless humiliation and despair was to get out. The division between "us" (the people) and "them" (the government) was complete.

The scene changes

By 1988 the regime was in a state of total paralysis. Wage increases could not keep pace with rocketing prices, and the government began to fear a campaign of massive civil disobedience. Discontent boiled over in April and then in August when strikes broke out in Gdansk and key industrial areas.

Walesa calmed the strikers and appealed, yet again, for the recognition of Solidarity. As confidence in the government reached an all-time low, his own prestige began to grow both at home and abroad. When allowed to argue Solidarity's case on television with the head of the official Trades Unions, he ran rings round his opponent.

The situation became increasingly untenable for

Jerzy Popieluszko, the young pro-Solidarity priest, who articulated the hopes and fears of the people during martial law. His murder by the secret police in October 1984 caused outrage and heartbreak. But there were many other victims too. The Polish Helsinki Committee, which monitored human rights violations, presented a horrifying list of kidnappings, beatings, torture and murder.

the government, and at last they had to turn for help to the despised "man of no importance". After stormy meetings with his Central Committee, General Jaruzelski summoned a round table conference. At the conference an impassioned Walesa gave voice to the discontents of the Poles.

Victory in sight

Bargaining was bitter and dragged on for weeks, but in the end a compromise was reached. Solidarity was made legal, and provision was made for a new Parliament to which opposition representatives could be elected. There had to be concessions, of course. Opposition members were still to be in a

> *"It's a bit like learning to do the long jump. First a little jump, then a little bit further. We thought we could do more than we were capable of doing, and we were beaten back. But we'll try again. You must have hope."*
>
> Lech Walesa.

Solidarity was banned. But the people did not forget; for another five years of repression, they waited and hoped for freedom. At every festival and every church service they remembered and showed their silent support. Lech Walesa waited too.

minority; and the key office of President would be reserved to a Party nominee. Nevertheless, hope was powerfully alive again in Poland.

June 1989 saw the first elections in Poland. Solidarity won an overwhelming majority of the votes. There is a long way to go to full democracy but if it is at last gaining a toe-hold, it is in no small measure thanks to Lech Walesa who never ceased to believe that full dialogue was possible. "In the end I shall not have waited in vain," he once said. "When the moment comes for dialogue, we must be ready and we must be united. And when that day comes, I am convinced that it is simply not possible for us not to win..."

"Lech Walesa has made humanity bigger and more inviolable. His two-edged good fortune is that he has won a victory which is not of this, our political, world. The presentation of the Peace Prize to him today is a homage to the power of victory which abides in one person's belief, in his vision, and in his courage to follow his call."
Egil Aarvik, Chairman of the Norwegian Nobel Committee.

59

Glossary

Aryans: Originally the name given to all descendants of the Indo-Europeans who were the theoretical first race from which most West European cultures and languages came. Perverted by *Hitler* to mean people with Nordic features (i.e. blond hair and blue eyes) who, he declared, were members of his "master-race".

B.B.C.: The British Broadcasting Corporation, which is the state-owned broadcasting network in the United Kingdom.

Bloc: A group of people, parties or nations united by a common interest.

Cold War: A state of political tension that exists between countries, in particular the U.S.S.R. and the U.S.A. The aim is to gain political and economic advantages without actually fighting and to influence countries not committed to either side.

Communism: The belief in the theory of common ownership of the means of production, distribution and supply by a classless society in which each person works according to ability and receives according to need. It is based on Karl Marx's belief that for there to be a more equal distribution of wealth, capitalism must be replaced by a working class government.

Conscription: The system under which all able-bodied men [and, in some countries, women] are legally required to serve with the armed forces.

Detente: The easing of tension in relations between countries.

Dissident: Someone who does not agree with the official government policy. In the Soviet *bloc*, dissidents are those who campaign for a more democratic and humanitarian approach. To avoid censorship, their material is circulated secretly.

Glasnost: A Russian term, literally meaning "openness". It is part of Mikhail Gorbachev's fundamental change of policy towards a fairer, less restricted country with better, more open relations with the rest of the world. Since his election in 1985, Gorbachev has stressed the need for glasnost both within the Soviet Union and in Soviet relations with Western countries.

Hard currency: A currency that is not likely to suddenly change in value, because it is constantly in demand and widely accepted. The U.S. dollar and pound sterling are examples.

Hitler, Adolf: (1889-1945) Born in Austria, he became leader of the *Nazi* party in Germany. While in prison after an attempted coup, he wrote "Mein Kampf" expressing his ideas of *Aryan* superiority and hatred of the Jews. He became dictator in 1934. By ordering the invasion of Poland in 1939, he started World War II. He killed himself in April 1945, when Berlin fell to the Russians, rather than face capture.

KOR: The Social Self-Defence Committee set up by a group of intellectuals in 1976. It provided legal and financial aid to workers who were unjustly punished by the police.

Liquidate: To arrange for someone to be killed.

Logo: The identifying symbol of an organization or publication.

Manifesto: A public statement outlining the principles, policies and intentions of an organization.

Marxist: Someone who follows the ideas of the two German philosophers, Karl Marx and Friedrich Engels. The term loosely describes any militant *communist*.

Master Race: see Aryans.

Morse Code: An international system of communication invented by Samuel Morse. Patterns of short and long signals are used to represent the letters of the alphabet and numbers.

Nazi: A member of the National Socialist German Workers' Party, which came to power in 1933 under the dictatorship of Adolf *Hitler*.

Nobel Prizes: The much respected annual prizes, awarded for outstanding world achievements in chemistry, physics, medicine, literature, peace and economics.

Partisan: A member of an armed group that operates in occupied territories during wars.

Pauper: Someone who is extremely poor and often dependent on public charity.

Perestroika: Literally meaning "restructuring", this is the term used by the Soviet leader, Mikhail Gorbachev, for the economic and government reforms he has initiated since coming to power in 1985.

Polish United Workers' Party: The ruling *communist* party, formed after Poland was declared a people's republic in 1947. It is usually referred to as the Party.

Red Army: The former name for the army of the *Soviet Union*. It was renamed the Soviet Army in 1946.

Reich: The name given to the government or territory of a German empire. Adolf *Hitler's Nazi* regime from 1933-45 was the Third Reich.

Solidarity: The name of the independent trades unions set up in Poland in 1980 under the leadership of Lech Walesa. It was formed after a series of strikes in the Baltic shipyards forced the authorities to allow trades unions, that were independent of *communist* party control, to exist.

Soviet Union: This is another name for the Union of Soviet Socialist Republics, U.S.S.R., which is made up of fifteen republics. The largest of these is the Russian Soviet Federal Socialist Republic, known as Russia. Today, the name Russia is usually used to describe the whole of the U.S.S.R.

Stalin, Joseph: (1879-1953) A Russian leader who was the virtual ruler of the *Soviet Union* by ordering the murder of all potential rivals and opponents in a series of purges in the 1930s. During his rule he transferred industry and agriculture from private to state ownership and *liquidated* the kulaks, the peasant landowners, who opposed this policy.

Warsaw Pact: An agreement for military alliance signed in Warsaw in 1955 by Albania, Bulgaria, Czechoslovakia, East Germany, Hungary, Poland, Romania and the U.S.S.R. Albania withdrew from the Pact in 1968 when the *Soviet Union* invaded Czechoslovakia.

ZOMO: The name for the Polish riot police.

Further Reading

Craig, Mary: *The Crystal Spirit, Lech Walesa and His Poland* (Coronet Books, London, 1988)
An adult biography of Lech Walesa by the author of this book. Very exciting and easy to read.

Michener, James: *Poland* (Corgi Books, London, 1987)
A long, adult book that gives an excellent feel of the historical background of Poland.

Sharman, Tim: *The Rise of Solidarity* (Wayland, Hove, 1986)
A school-book that gives a concise political background to Lech Walesa's story.

Walesa, Lech: *A Path of Hope* (Collins Harvill, London, 1987)
A difficult, adult book, but vital for serious students.

Important Dates

1918   After centuries of repeated occupations by Russia and Germany, Poland is revived as an independent republic.

1939   Sept 1: Germany invades Poland.
Sept 3: Britain and France declare war on Germany.
World War II has begun.
Sept 17: The Soviet Union invades Poland.

1943   Sept: Lech's father is taken prisoner by the Germans.
Sept 29: Lech Walesa is born in Popowo, Poland.

1944   The German Army is driven out of Poland by Soviet force. Poland is under Soviet domination.

1945   March: Lech's father is freed.
May: Lech's father dies.
July: Poland's boundaries are redrawn at the Potsdam Conference.

1947   Poland is declared a communist people's republic.

1948   The Polish United Workers' Party is formed.

1956   The Poznan food riots. Wladyslaw Gomulka is installed as leader of the Polish United Workers' Party.

1959   Lech, aged sixteen, starts a three-year course at the Trade School in Lipno.

1963   Lech is conscripted into the Polish Army for two years' military service.

1967   May: Lech, aged twenty-three, arrives in Gdansk and starts work at the Lenin shipyard.

1968   March: Student riots are suppressed by the authorities. Thirty thousand students are sent into exile.

1969   Nov 8: Lech Walesa, aged twenty-six, marries Danuta Golos.

1970   Dec 12: The government announces drastic increases in the price of food and fuel. A state of emergency is declared after violence and strikes break out in the Baltic towns of Gdansk and Gdynia. Edward Gierek replaces Wladyslaw Gomulka as leader of the Polish United Workers' Party.

1976   Feb: Lech loses his job at the shipyard after speaking out against the authorities.
Gierek announces further increases in the price of food. Violence breaks out in Ursus and Radom. The KOR is set up.

1978   April 29: The Baltic Committee for Free and Independent Trade Unions is set up by Lech and other dissident workers.
Oct: Cardinal Karol Wojtyla of Cracow becomes Pope John Paul II.

1979   June: Pope John Paul II visits Poland.
Dec 16: Seven thousand people gather at the shipyard in Gdansk to remember those killed in 1970. Lech calls on them to set up independent groups to protect themselves.

1980   Aug: Lech calls for an immediate occupation-strike at the Lenin shipyard in Gdansk.

Aug 23: Lech has talks with Deputy Prime Minister Jagielski.
Aug 31: The Gdansk Agreement is signed. Independent trades unions are now allowed to exist.
Sept: Stanislaw Kania replaces Edward Gierek as party leader.
Nov: Solidarity is registered as an independent trade union, the first in a Soviet-controlled country.

1981   Jan: Lech meets Pope John Paul II in Rome.
Mar: Security police beat up Solidarity members during a meeting in Bydogoszcz.
May-June: Lech visits Japan, Switzerland and France.
Sept: Solidarity holds first National Congress.
Oct: Stanislaw Kania resigns as party leader and is replaced by General Wojciech Jaruzelski.
Nov 4: Lech meets General Jaruzelski and Cardinal Glemp for talks.
Nov 25: ZOMO riot police break up a student sit-in in Warsaw.
Dec 12: Solidarity leaders are rounded up.
Dec 13: General Jaruzelski imposes a state of martial law and declares Solidarity illegal. Lech begins a year-long internment.

1982   May 3: ZOMO riot squads attack a crowd of demonstrators and arrest over one thousand.
Aug 31: First anniversary of the Gdansk Agreement. Trouble flares up all over the country.
Nov: Lech is released from internment.

1983   April: Lech returns to work at the Lenin shipyard.
June: Lech meets Pope John Paul II during his second visit to Poland.
Dec: Lech Walesa is awarded the Nobel Peace Prize.

1984   Oct: Father Jerzy Popieluszko is murdered by the security forces.

1986   July: The authorities announce a general amnesty. Twenty thousand detainees are released.

1987   June: Pope John Paul II's third visit to Poland.

1989   Jan: Two pro-Solidarity priests, Father Stanislaw Suchowolec and Father Stefan Niedzielak are found dead.
Feb 6: Lech opens talks in Warsaw between the government and Solidarity.
April 17: Solidarity is legalized.
June: Poland's first elections are held in two parts on June 4 and June 18. These are the first partly-democratic elections in Eastern Europe/Soviet bloc since 1945. As laid down at the Round Table Conference, the Solidarity opposition are allowed to contest thirty-five per cent (161) of seats for the Lower House. In a landslide victory, they win *160 seats*. In elections for the Upper House, the Solidarity opposition wins all 100 seats.
Sept 24: Following the failure of the Communist party to form a government, a Prime Minister from the Solidarity party is appointed by the Lower House – the first non-Communist government in Eastern Europe for forty-five years.

Index